REACHING THE
GOAL

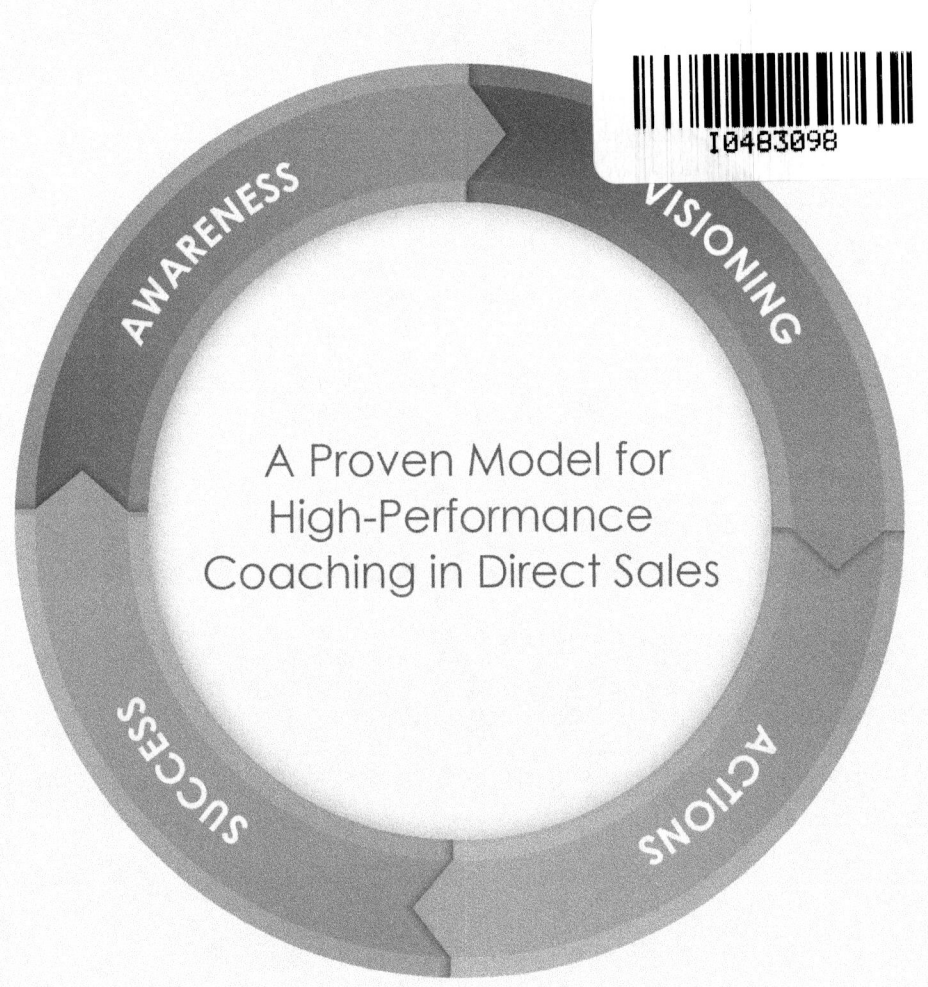

AWARENESS

VISIONING

A Proven Model for
High-Performance
Coaching in Direct Sales

SUCCESS

ACTIONS

TERRI KELLY

ISBN: 1497402875
ISBN 13: 9781497402874

ACKNOWLEDGEMENTS

I'd like to thank all of my clients from the past 15 years, and all the companies worked for prior, for giving me the opportunity to think outside the box and create tools, processes, techniques, etc. that has led me to the development of the coaching model and all the tools that are presented in this book and workbook.

Thank you to a few of my lifelong friends that have provided encouragement and support throughout the years and have always believed I could do great things: Debbie Lawrence, John Michala, Steve Tanury, Jim Mongrain, Lee Hayward, Rose Pelot, Lisa Perkins, Mary Hubble, Colleen Topper, Carol Josifovski, and Shawna Hicks-Cranston. I know there are others and I appreciate all of you as well.

Special thanks, from the bottom of my heart, to Nicole Brake — without your assistance and support of this project this book would not be published.

PREFACE

Reading this book is the closest thing possible to having a series of sessions with a great coach. I can give no absolute guarantees, but I feel certain that *Reaching the Goal* will help you find exactly what you want and need to take your communication and problem-solving effectiveness to the next level. Along with your own considerable inner and business resources, you can use the model I've taught for many years and outlined for you here to reach your goals.

You may be thinking, "Another book about 'coaching'? Just what the business world needs!" Yes, since the 80's, the style of managing people began transforming, experimentally, into a more sports-type approach where the buzz words "team" and "teamwork" and "coach" took hold. But running a business is not exactly analogous to striving for a winning season, and in an organization, every team member must be highly productive, every day – no one just sits on the bench. So business coaching is different, and this book spells out exactly how to draw from other approaches, but use the one (the one you are about to learn) which has been proven to be effective in all organization large and small.

You may be saying, "What makes Terri Kelly an expert on 'effective coaching'?" Well, my 30-plus years of human resources, organizational development, corporate training, consulting, and coaching experience, of which half has been as an entrepreneur. Through the work I delivered to small and large (fortune 500) clients I always went to my core – coaching – and used those skills during my engagements.

Through the years my clients, colleagues, and friends always suggested to me that I write a book. Secretly I have always had the desire to write a book but the fear of "how?" and "who did I think I was to write a book?" always kept me from getting on with the writing and publishing. What changed? First I had lunch with a client several months ago who shared that his organization (a large car manufacturer) was still using the tools and resources I had developed and implemented for them 10 years ago. The client further stated my work "held the test of time." The next week, I received a call from one of my fortune 500 clients in Chicago who said he was not sure if I was aware of the powerful impact I had on their organization when I was there consulting, delivering coaching workshops, and individual coaching sessions to their managers. He went on to say that after five years, the organization was still using all the coaching material, and that the culture had truly been transformed from "tell–do" to "coaching" as a preferred management style. Following these encounters, I decided I would put my simple, yet powerful, coaching model to work, write a book, and share it with the world.

Through my walk in corporate America as an employee and later as a consultant, I have found that one crucial success factor stands out as one so simple, yet the most difficult at the same time to conquer, that being communication. While management may agree in theory, studies have shown that management doesn't realize that they are not communicating with non-management. Management spends a tremendous amount of time in meetings with each other, discussing problems, sharing opportunities, and learning what is happening outside their domain, and then they assume everyone else knows what they know. This holds true in all size companies and environments. However, when provided an efficient and effective model with a logical step-by-step method, leaders quickly improve communication at all levels and the results are immediate and often dramatic.

The simple coaching model teaches people how to create a safe place for people to come and problem-solve. Practicing the coaching model will enhance the behaviors of support, commitment, encouragement, development, and feedback. Consistently exhibiting these behaviors will provide alignment of goals, motivation of others, and increased capabilities. These effects all have one thing in common, "better communication". This inevitably means improved performance and a higher Return on Investment.

Why is the coaching model so simple to apply? I have removed all the noise. What do I mean by "removed all the noise"? I have designed a step-by-step process that allows an individual or team to move beyond problem solving into action planning, and to measuring success every step along the way. What becomes extremely useful is "what you measure is critical." Therefore, your action plan provides the road map for what you and your team focus on to be successful and to move the organization forward. Many managers and businesses get caught up in measuring the wrong thing. The simple coaching model taught in this book and workbook provides you with tools and a process to get unstuck in any situation, and to create action to achieve desired measurable results.

Learning to be a great coach and to make the transformation from "tell–do" to "coaching" as a preferred leadership style will allow you to create a company that values engagement, collaboration, and communication. Your organization will exhibit higher morale, better quality, less turnover, and higher performance. People in your organization will feel significant and will share how proud they are to work for with you. What better testimonial than your team communicating to family, friends, customers and potential customers what a great product/service your company delivers and they thoroughly enjoy working for with you.

So I encourage you to read on, I know you can become a great Coach!

PROLOGUE

The nagging sound of the alarm clock woke Wendy from her slumber. She stirred and stretched, willing the clock to silence itself. Knowing that the buzz would wake everyone in the house, Wendy slipped her arm from beneath the warmth of her comforter to silence the alarm. She would give anything to sleep in – just once – but, alas, duty called and this morning Wendy was an "opener". As her feet hit the floor Wendy wondered what she may encounter today – after all, she worked retail and it was Saturday.

Wendy was a wife, mother, and college graduate. She was everything to everyone and often cared for herself last. Sam was a successful business man that encouraged Wendy to be a stay-at-home mom for the boys when they were young. She was grateful that she had the opportunity to watch their sons grow, but when they no longer needed her full-time Wendy decided that she wanted to work. She needed something for her. Knowing that her degree was worthy but that finding a job as a graphic designer would be tough, Wendy weighed her options and did what every smart woman would do – applied for positions where she shopped and would receive the best discount!

The first year went by quickly and was relatively painless. Wendy enjoyed meeting new people, helping customers, and a decent discount on items that she would have purchased at full price. The biggest drawback was the uncertainly of her schedule, but she knew that the job would have ups and downs. Wendy learned to roll with the punches and never complained. Sure, she missed a few of her son's basketball games, but her neighbor happily recorded them for her.

As time went on, Wendy realized that she was beginning to miss more and more activities with her children and time with her husband and friends. She found the summer months particularly difficult because the boys were on break from school. They were old enough to care for themselves, but Wendy missed spending days at the lake and evenings by the bonfire. Then came a crushing reality – Wendy was spending almost her entire paycheck before it hit their bank account. Sam continued to support her and her desire to work, but Wendy no longer felt that retail was her cup of tea.

Sam's position at the bank was intact but the economy was taking its toll on his salary. They could no longer afford some of the luxuries they had become accustomed to, they were over their head in debt for the first time, they were upside down in their mortgage, and they had children that continued to grow and have needs that had to be met. They were in uncharted waters and they were nervous. All of this stress and pressure was taking a toll on their marriage and the tension in the house was thick.

Wendy decided to make a change. She wasn't sure what that change would entail, but this was the last Saturday she would slip from the house quietly as her family slept. Wendy went through the motions at work and watched the clock intently, wishing the time away. Customers filtered in and out of the store at a typical Saturday pace. Most were just browsing, but Wendy recognized a few regular shoppers that she always enjoyed helping.

Megan, a store regular, had become one of Wendy's favorite customers. They had children in the same school and they often chatted about life, husbands, and raising children in this tough world. As luck would have it, Megan entered the store just as Wendy was punching out for the day. Megan had a great disposition and seemed to have her life in order; she always wore a smile. Wendy wanted that; she wanted the outlook on life that Megan had.

Megan once told Wendy what she did for work and how direct sales had entered her life at just the right time. Upon her return home, Wendy decided to do some internet searching and see what information she could uncover. She visited several sites and found that all offered great earning potential and full training. Going with her gut, she enrolled with a company she knew offered products that many of her friends would purchase. As she clicked the "confirm enrollment" link on the webpage, Wendy let out a huge sigh of relief and grinned from ear to ear.

A few days later Wendy's enrollment kit arrived in the mail. She had given her boss her two weeks' notice and while they were sad to see her go, they understood that she needed a new challenge. Wendy opened her kit with enthusiasm and immediately popped the welcome CD into her computer. She could really work at home, have coffee or lunch with friends, host parties, and still make money? It looked so easy…almost too good to be true!

With the purchase of her enrollment kit Wendy received free training from one of the company's top sellers. The training could also be done from the comfort of her own home and at her convenience. She opened her planner and added training dates to next week's agenda. She knew that working from home was going to require just as much dedication and self-discipline as any nine-to-five - if not MORE! - and she would need to remain organized.

The following week Wendy completed the online training. The program really did look simple and it seemed as if the product would sell itself. Wendy began calling friends to see who would be interested in hosting a party. Her friends seemed enthused, but many were hesitant to commit because of summer travel and vacation plans. They all said that maybe having a party in the fall would work out better because their families would be back into their typical routines. Wendy hoped that they were right; maybe summer was a bad time to give up her income and become self-employed!

As summer came to a close, Wendy's frustrations grew. Maybe she was in over her head. The training that she received was minimal, nothing more than just a pep talk, but how could she be spirited about this if she couldn't make any sales. Parties created the revenue and she couldn't find a hostess willing to open her home for one evening. One evening – that was all she was asking! First it was summer travel plans, then back-to-school activities and fall sports, and now the hustle and bustle of the holidays. Wendy was about to throw in the towel!

Frustrated, Wendy returned to her company's website to read through the blogs and see what others were doing to be successful. Surely she wasn't the only one struggling – or was she? She sure felt alone. It all looked so simple and yet she hadn't even recouped her funds for the enrollment kit. As she perused the company blog, a side banner ad caught her attention: TAKE ACTION! COMMUNICATE CLEARLY! SET GOALS! INCREASE PRODUCTIVITY! BE A GREAT LEADER! CREATE

A SUCCESSFUL SALES TEAM! GAIN A VIRTUAL COACH! A team...that was it! Megan once told her that the fastest way to grow as an independent seller was to create a network. Wendy needed to create a team.

Click-click-click, Wendy sought the registration information. She was delighted to see that the program was both affordable, and was being held in a nearby city. In excitement, she filled out the online registration for the seminar. Once she had her sales team in place, she would be unstoppable. Her enthusiasm for success was returning and she was, again, excited about the potential.

Though excited about the course, doubt was constant; would her knowledge base be enough? Would she know what they were talking about? Would she fit in with the others taking the course? HOT market, WARM market, COLD Market; Prospecting; Organizing and Time Management; Setting Appointments; Compliance with company systems; Long and short term goals; and Overcoming Objections. Could she learn and implement it all? Would it make a difference? And, most importantly, could it improve her chances of being successful? Could she FINALLY gain the freedom and peace of mind she wanted after leaving her retail job?

As she drove through town the Saturday morning of training she sure hoped she was ready; her heart and her mind were racing!

Fortunately, Wendy, like you, discovered the secrets in this book, this new approach to problem-solving which made all the difference. Certainly, her hard work and determination were important factors in her success, but what really sealed the deal was her introduction to this step-by-step coaching model, which is outlined, detailed, and illustrated in this book. Following this model, Wendy overcame her troubles---and so can you!

Learning and applying this model can help you more efficiently and effectively solve problems in your business and in your life. Wherever you are today, that starting place is perfect. Whether your small business is up and running or you are building a team of independent sales representatives and have just started, this book is for you. Follow Wendy, and this step-by-step guide to better communication and increased sales.

Let's get started.

HOPE FOR THE TEAM

The Monday morning following Wendy's completion of the Coaching seminar was the day Wendy re-committed to her direct sales job. Armed with new knowledge, and knowing she always had her "virtual coach" with her on her iPad, Wendy created a vision board. It was much easier to put her ideas on paper now that she knew the potential afforded her by her new company. She established her personal goals, created goals for team she was going to create, and then created personal goals for each member of the team. Wendy became increasingly excited as she watched her vision boards develop.

At the heart of Wendy's vision boards were several ideas: using a positive approach, building relationships, staying compliant with the newly-written company protocol and procedures, closing the sale, and inspiring others.

Let's walk through Wendy's vision and see just where it takes us.

AN INTRODUCTION TO COACHING

What is Coaching?

Chances are, you already have a clear mental image about what coaching entails, perhaps in a sports-related context. If so, you may be wondering: how can this image be applied to my business to achieve success? Beyond the clear connection between a team sport and a team business, the practice of coaching has plenty to offer today's small business owner.

Let's start with the most basic of basics: what does it mean to be a coach, or to perform the act of coaching? The base definition is "a teaching, training, or a development process via which an individual is supported while achieving a specific personal or professional result or goal." That's coaching in the broadest sense; over the course of this book, we'll stick with a more focused interpretation. As far as we're concerned, coaching simply means using open communication to achieve a desired result. This "communication" will often take place between different individuals, as you might expect, but it can also be an internal process—self-communication can sometimes lead to the strongest results of all!

Of course, every situation is different, and one person's preferred (and most effective) interpretation of coaching could vary from another. Perhaps it would be best if we step back a bit, and identify coaching by its key traits. What qualities are common to any good coaching strategy, and what would rule it out? Let's take a look:

WHAT COACHING IS AND WHAT COACHING IS NOT!

➤ Coaching has roots in behavioral science (psychology), athletics, and corporate training

➤ Coaching focuses on the present and helps people move forward toward the future

COACHING IS	COACHING IS NOT
➤ Action-oriented	➤ Giving advice
➤ Focused on the future	➤ Counseling
➤ Goal-oriented	➤ Fixing people
➤ Dedicated to growth and success	➤ Doing it for them
➤ Asking questions	➤ Policing

As we saw from the standard definition, coaching's a pretty big and open-ended concept. There are many ways to interpret what coaching means for you, but some will be more productive than others. When you visualize yourself coaching in the business sphere, here are some images to strive for, as well as a few to avoid:

COACHING IS NOT:

- **GIVING ADVICE OR COUNSELING.** Thinking back on the sports image, a coach is purely a leader or mentor figure, right? Not according to our definition! Certainly, coaching will call upon you to take plenty of responsibility and initiative, but don't think of it as a one-way street. Our vision of coaching encourages all involved parties to learn from one another and work back and forth towards a universal solution.

- FIXING PEOPLE, DOING IT FOR THEM OR POLICING. A few famous coaches are pretty rough around the edges, but they do apparently get the job done. Bobby Knight didn't exactly have the most pleasant demeanor, but Indiana sure did win a lot with him at the helm. Surely you've got to be tough on people to get results? Not so! We consider coaching to be a team process, built on a foundation of respect and transparency. Most of all, it will challenge you to take responsibility for any problems at hand—projecting them onto others will do more harm than good.

Aggressive coaching -- good for basketball, maybe not so much for business.
Image via **Flickr** by Benji Panic

COACHING IS:

- **ACTION ORIENTED.** Initially, coaching is all about communication, but the ultimate point of that communication is to inspire action. Coaching is about understanding how things currently are, determining how you want to change things or move things forward, and then *working to make that change happen.*

- **FOCUSED ON THE FUTURE.** As a coach, you should always face forward. Be aware of your present situation, but don't become bogged down in it—keep moving towards the future scenario you desire.

- **GOAL ORIENTED.** You shouldn't expect success to come right away, nor should you rush forward without having a clear destination in mind. Setting a series of reasonable, attainable goals will keep you going at a steady, satisfying pace, and help you work your way towards a greater final result.

- **ASKING QUESTIONS.** Fundamentally, coaching will rely on plenty of reflection, both on yourself and on your business. To effectively move forward, you've got to have a firm grasp on all the relevant information. Remember this important rule—if you don't know something, never be afraid to ask!

- **DEDICATED TO GROWTH AND SUCCESS.** We left this one for last, because it's probably the most important. It may not seem like much, but a good attitude will go a long way on your path to success. Stay optimistic, and keep aiming for that positive result!

If this feels like a lot to take in at once, don't worry—we've broken down our coaching model into a step-by-step process, and we'll guide you through it every step of the way.

A Step-by-Step Guide to Coaching

In a nutshell, our process can be understood as six simple steps, each of which comes with its own set of questions:

1. Identify your TOPIC—what is the problem, or what do you want to improve?

2. Examine the CURRENT REALITY—what's working, what isn't?

3. Imagine your VISION—what does your ideal scenario look like?

4. Define SUCCESS—how will you know when you've achieved a desired result, and what can you use to make it happen?

5. Design a plan of ACTION (utilizing available RESOURCES)—what will you do to achieve success, with whom, and when?

6. Prepare for OBSTACLES—what could get in the way, and how will you overcome it?

Represented graphically, the process looks something like this:

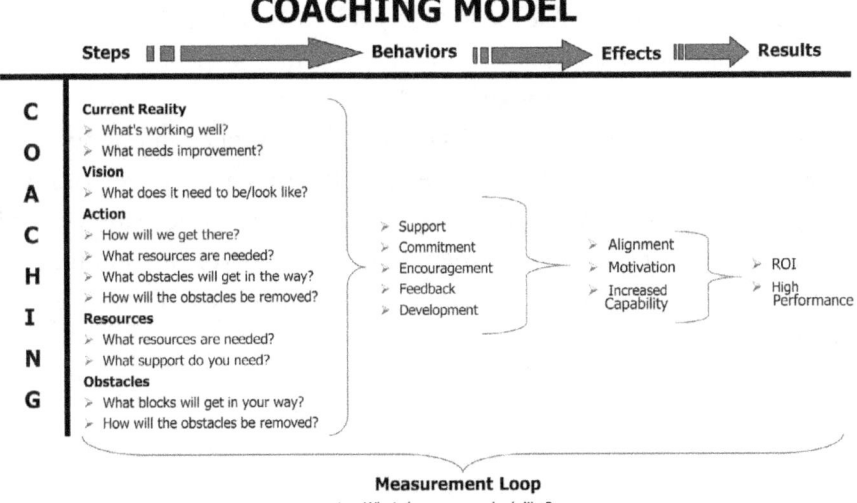

We will return to this model later on in the book, after we've covered each individual step. For now, focus on the key questions—once you've gathered information and answered them; you're ready to take action. Carry out your plans, and work towards the success you defined!

After you've followed your plan and seen the results, it's time to reflect once more. Did you achieve the success you envisioned? If not, try going back to the drawing board, and come up with a new plan of attack. Above all, don't get discouraged! Just because you haven't yet achieved success doesn't mean you've failed; on the contrary, you've had a valuable learning experience, which you can use to build towards your eventual triumph.

If you do achieve success, congratulations! You've worked hard and deserve plenty of recognition for it. However, you needn't stop just yet. How much further can coaching take you? Truly, you don't need to set any limits—design a new plan for an even greater success, and work your way even higher!

Aim for Success!

Again, if it seems like things are moving too fast or are oversimplified, don't worry—we'll cover everything in full detail, step-by-step, chapter-by-chapter. For now, above all, stay positive! Even if you feel completely stuck, frustrated, and behind in your business, no problem is too insurmountable for a sensible coaching plan to conquer. Never give up hope—with responsible analysis and a deliberate step-by-step process, success will be well within your reach!

As we walk you through each step, feel free to follow along with our custom-made coaching worksheet (seen on the following page), or if you prefer, give it a try on your own after reading. Along the way, we'll fill it in ourselves, using our friend Wendy as an example. Beyond that, for more coaching tips, techniques, aids, and so on, you can download and browse our supplemental workbook.

RESULTS-BASED COACHING MODEL

Action Planning Template

TOPIC	WHAT ARE WE GOING TO BE WORKING ON? WHAT PROBLEM DO YOU NEED TO SOLVE?	

CURRENT REALITY	WHAT IS WORKING WELL?	WHAT NEEDS IMPROVEMENT?

VISION	WHAT DOES IT NEED TO BE / LOOK LIKE?

SUCCESS	WHAT DOES SUCCESS LOOK LIKE? HOW DO YOU KNOW YOU HAVE GOTTEN THE RESULT YOU WANT?

ACTION	WHAT ARE YOU GOING TO DO?	WITH WHOM?	WHEN?

OBSTACLES	WHAT COULD GET IN THE WAY?	HOW WILL YOU OVERCOME IT?

COACHING BEHAVIORS AND SKILLS

Attended Webinar Seminar

Realizing that her earning potential was now directly related to how hard she worked and the team she created, Wendy was determined to be focused and driven. She decided that asking her friends to be part of her team wasn't the best option. Maybe she should venture out, meet new people, and create a team of people that have the same desire as her. All of her friends were pretty consumed with their own families, dreams, and goals.

Within a short time she was able to put a small team together. Her team didn't have to be large in numbers; they just needed to all be hard workers in search of a common goal. Everyone got along well on the surface, but Wendy could tell that there were kinks to work out. She saw personality conflicts and sales tactics that didn't mesh, but she wasn't willing to give up.

Wanting to create harmony amongst the group, Wendy searched the internet for words of encouragement and advice. There was certainly a large community of direct sales people and there must be a virtual place they go to discuss what works and what doesn't work.

Purely by accident, Wendy stumbled upon a website about success. The type of success wasn't immediately identifiable and, at this point, Wendy didn't care because she was intrigued by one simple word: **Coaching**. If she was going to lead a team, she would need to be a coach!

The Right Tools for the Job

At this point, we're just about ready to begin planning out your long-term coaching strategy. Before we fully delve into that process, though, let's go over some of the basic behaviors and skills you'll need to exhibit and practice to succeed in your coaching plan. The reason we'll be spending a chapter covering these concepts in advance is that these qualities will be a fundamental part of the whole coaching process, every step of the way. Practice these behaviors and skills well, as they'll prove instrumental in resolving problems, moving your business forward, and achieving your desired results.

Support

While one can certainly apply the principles we're covering to a solo scenario (perhaps involving introspective question-and-answer sessions), we'll mainly focus on coaching as a one-on-one activity—though it can also work very well if applied to a team, as well. No matter how many people are involved, coaching aims to bring out the best in everyone for the greater good of the collective. Support means ensuring that everyone, including you, contributes what's needed for the good of the company.

As a coach, be prepared to analyze your own and your teammates' capabilities, and ask yourself what kind of input you can provide. If a teammate is struggling, don't hesitate to support them in any way you can—acknowledging any shortfalls and working together to overcome them is a much better response than simply leaving the person behind. You're all in this together!

Commitment

Coaching doesn't have to be a difficult process, but it does take time, consistency, and persistence. It's very good to be optimistic about growth and the general future, but keep in mind that achieving your goals will take patience and commitment.

When you create your long-term coaching plan, be prepared to commit—most of the effects will take time to become visible, and you'll need to be prepared to measure success along the way. If a new idea hasn't yet produced the results you want, try giving it a little more time to develop. Of course, some ideas may not pan out, either. If an idea has had time to work, yet still hasn't bloomed like you'd hoped, it's perfectly reasonable to try a different approach—your strongest commitment, after all, should be to get a positive result. Continuously moving forward is the key.

Engagement

Basically, practicing good engagement means understanding your own abilities and role within the coaching plan, and applying yourself fully to carry it out. Though this behavior focuses on the individual level, it has an important effect on your team dynamic, as well. Ideally, you want your own actions to serve as a model for your fellow team members—by staying positive, motivated, and engaged, you can inspire your team to follow your example. Once everyone's committed to full engagement, success won't be far off!

Development

As the above behaviors have indicated, coaching has a lot to do with identifying your strengths, as well as those of your team, and using them effectively. However, it pays quite a bit to understand your weaknesses, as well. Don't think of these aspects so much as purely negative qualities, or as problems that hold you back; consider them more like areas with a higher potential for improvement, or obstacles to be carefully navigated around. Naturally, facing forward and focusing on development, or accentuating your strengths and improving in other respects, is a direct means of improving your business on the whole.

Feedback

Make no mistake about it: all of the behaviors we've gone over so far will be very useful to your coaching efforts. That said, if we were to settle on just one most important quality, we'd have to zoom in on all things related to feedback. Being able to properly give, receive, and make use of feedback is the surest indicator of a strong, forward-thinking team dynamic.

What makes feedback so crucial to coaching and business growth? That's a pretty big subject, so let's break it up and tackle the basic questions, one at a time:

WHAT IS FEEDBACK?

In brief, feedback is the most direct means of interpersonal problem-solving. Basically, it involves one person commenting on the effort of another, pointing out strengths and weaknesses. When all sides involved do their part responsibly and transparently, the feedback process is the best tried-and-true method of finding areas in need of improvement, as well as providing encouragement and praise.

Feedback does involve a major emphasis on highlighting needs for improvement, since it's a very effective method for finding such things. However, feedback is not the same as criticism, nor should it be used as such. If you have to point out a negative, don't sugar-coat it, but don't hit the person over the head with it, either. Nobody likes to be told they're doing something wrong—keep your approach direct, but gentle. Be responsible and respectful with your feedback, and you'll receive a response in kind.

WHY GIVE FEEDBACK?

We give feedback to:

- Recognize and reward effort. If a person has been performing well, giving them recognition will create a major incentive to keep up the good work. Furthermore, you can say specifically what you liked or what's working well, so as to fine-tune their performance even further.

- Improve quality. Regular, honest feedback will keep a person's performance improving at a steady rate, and prevent the person from forming bad habits or falling into a pattern.

- Build and maintain relationships. Feedback is a fundamental form of open, honest dialogue, which is essential to a constructive working relationship. Building an environment where feedback can be given openly will create a positive working climate, naturally inspiring trust and support amongst your team members.

- Clarify expectations. When people have a job to do, more often than not, they'll prefer to know exactly what to do and how to do it. Giving reliable feedback will create that understanding in your teammates, eliminating any potential guesswork or grey areas. The more open you are about your expectations, the more likely others are to be able to meet them.

HOW DO I GIVE FEEDBACK?

There are many ways to approach this topic, but here are some important tips to keep in mind:

- Be honest and open about your expectations, and be very clear about how they are or aren't being met. The less ambiguity you leave in this area, the more likely the person will be to benefit from your feedback.

- Focus on a mutual commitment rather than a strict leader-follower dynamic. Emphasizing the need to work together on an issue will communicate your level of engagement and willingness to support your peers. Don't simply point out another worker's flaws and order them around; similarly, don't be afraid to receive feedback from them, as well.

- Acknowledge positive performance, even if (perhaps especially if) your intended focus is to point out room for improvement. You want your teammates to look forward to receiving feedback and be motivated enough to use it well, both of which are more likely to happen if you pay attention to positives. In addition, highlighting positives will make any constructive feedback significantly easier both to give and receive.

- Frame it as an ongoing process. Just like the growth of your company, the growth of an individual is a long-term process that will encompass many, many feedback sessions. Be realistic in your expectations, and make it clear that you're fully invested in the person's ongoing improvement.

Feedback should be tailored to your specific situation, so the shape it takes will be quite unique to your circumstances. That said, you can always start with the foundation of a particular model. For starters, using personal "I" language goes a long way. Examine the chart below:

HOW TO GIVE CONSTRUCTIVE FEEDBACK EXAMPLE

"When you . . .   "When you are late to team meetings,

"I feel . . .   "I get irritated . . .

"Because I . . .   "Because I think it is wasting the time
                          of all the other team members and we
                          are never able to get through all the
                          agenda items."

Pause for Discussion

"I would like . . .   "I would like you to consider finding
                          some way of planning your schedule
                          that lets you get to these team meetings
                          on time."

"Because . . .   "Because that way we can be more
                          productive at the team meetings and
                          we can all keep to our tight schedules.

On the left are steps for framing your feedback, or good sentence starters; on the right are examples of their practical use. Feel free to experiment a bit as you grow more comfortable with the process, but in the early going, aim to hit all of these talking points in the right order, and you'll be in great shape.

Giving feedback can be a delicate process, and mastering the art will take some time. Still, if you aim to succeed in business—and general interpersonal interaction, for that matter—you'll need to put in the time and effort to make it a regular part of your routine.

There are many skills and behaviors that will prove important in your quest for business growth. It may seem like a lot to absorb, but if you're feeling overwhelmed don't worry too much about mastering everything right at this moment. This coaching process is designed to naturally call upon these skills and bring them out in you. Following the steps is as much about personal growth as it is about business success—jump on in, and aim for the top!

Once you've had a bit of practice, you may wish to consult some further reading. If so, we've got you covered! More tips, techniques, and tools can be found in our downloadable workbook.

IDENTIFY YOUR TOPIC

Independent Contributor vs Teamwork

Wendy had finished the workshop "Reaching the Goal: A Proven Model for High Performance Coaching with Sales Teams."

Feeling a bit overwhelmed about where to start, she thumbed through all of the handouts she had printed from the workshop about **Coaching**. She found her answer, as expected, right near the beginning.

"Ah, that's right," she said. "Figuring out the **Topic**!"

The Topic at Hand

This one's a short step, but it's quite important! Your topic may be big or small, but either way, it will determine the direction you'll take for every step to come.

Your first task is to sit down and start brainstorming. What, more than anything, is the main problem you're trying to solve? Try to keep it as simple as possible—you should be able to effectively sum it up in a single sentence, or better yet, a phrase. For this particular step, it will also help to be more broad than specific. Since you'll be basing all of the coming steps on the topic you establish, you might find you have a bit more freedom later on if you keep things open to interpretation now.

It will perhaps be easiest if you think of your topic as being synonymous with your goal. For example, you might be interested in using coaching to attract new clients to your business. That's perfectly fine—your topic could then be "Attracting new clients," or could be something closely related, such as "Improving visibility."

Though, as mentioned, your topic will stick with you for some time, it isn't necessarily set in stone. There are several reasons why you might be inclined to change the topic in the future—circumstances could change in a way you hadn't expected, your efforts might uncover a previously-unseen issue that seems more pressing, or, best-case-scenario, your plan could succeed and allow you to reach your goal or solve the problem. In cases like these, it certainly makes sense to go back and start the process again with a fresh topic. Just don't be too quick to do this without a good reason! At the very least, consider sticking with your old topic until you've finished filling out the coaching worksheet.

People, Process, and Safety

Our coaching process is meant to be extremely flexible, potentially focusing on topics of all conceivable sorts. Thus, an experienced user can, with only a slight bit of tweaking at most, adapt the model to any situation. To the first-timer, though, this freedom can actually become a creative roadblock right away. If you can use practically anything for your topic, how can you narrow it down to just one distinct concept at a time?

In these sorts of situations, it can be particularly helpful to think in terms of categories. If you can approach a problem by first organizing it into a defined group, it will keep you clear and focused on what sort of issue you're working with. We've found that many coaching-appropriate concerns can be neatly sorted into three major categories: **People**, **Process**, and **Safety**. Of course, as emphasized above, coaching can apply to many more situations, and the advanced user is encouraged to branch out and experiment, but we recommend that new users focus on the following model:

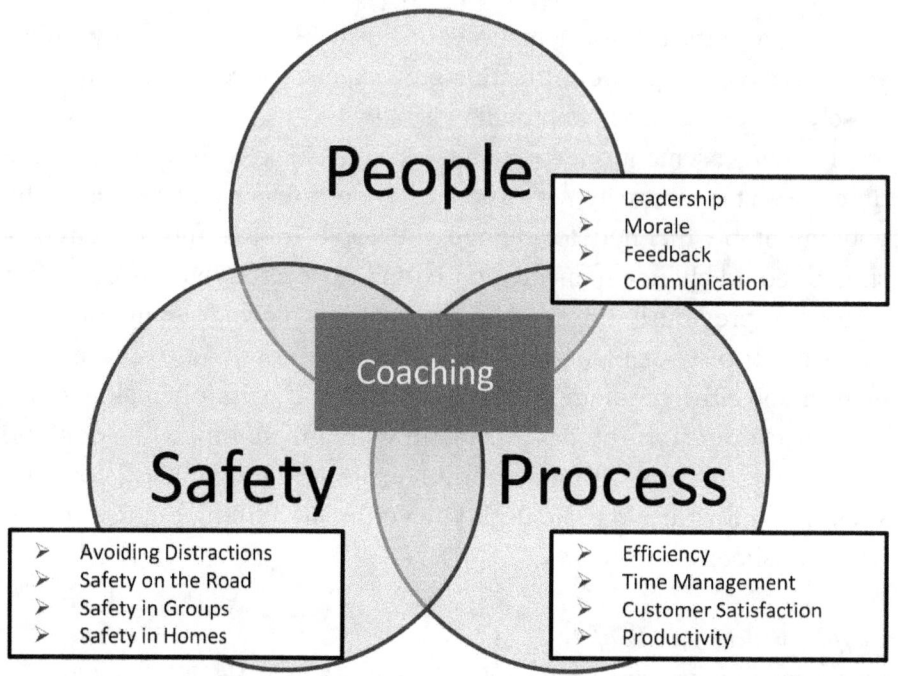

If you're having trouble narrowing down your ideas into one topic, try starting with one of these categories, and think of a few concepts that fit in those guidelines. Consider some of these examples as thought-starters:

PEOPLE: COMMUNICATION AND INTERPERSONAL INTERACTION

- Improving relationships with prospects, teammates, and colleagues

- Becoming a better listener

- Speaking more effectively in team meetings and group settings

- Understanding and working through cultural differences

- Being seen as a team player and inspiring the same in others

PROCESS: WORKPLACE PRODUCTIVITY, EFFICIENCY, AND EFFECTIVENESS

- Project management

- Data-driven planning and measuring results

- Reducing wasteful activities or behaviors

- Better meeting customer needs

- Improving turnaround time on projects or production

SAFETY: MAINTAINING A POSITIVE, HEALTHY WORK ENVIRONMENT

- Avoid distractions by planning our each day

- Safety on the road by not texting or reading while driving

- Maintain your car so it is in good running condition

- Home safety both in your own home office and those of prospects by communication about pets, children, and home belongings

Any one of these would make an excellent topic for a worksheet and coaching session. If you're stuck, imagine you had to deal with one of the above issues, and think about how you might go through the worksheet with it in mind. You can also follow along with Wendy's progress through her worksheet throughout this book, observing how her thoughts develop over the course of the process.

As a final note, for even more ideas and examples of the coaching process in action, remember to download and check out our coaching workbook!

Independent Contributor vs Teamwork – Continued

Wendy brainstormed about her **Topic** for some time, but found herself stuck.

"This coaching thing sure is hard," she sighed. "If only I had some help. Wait, wasn't there something like that in the workshop?"

She browsed through her notes, and spotted a note previously over-looked: Virtual Coach. Intrigued, she booted it up. After a few moments, a box popped up, prompting her for her name. She typed in "Wendy," and checked a box to enable "speech mode."

"Good evening, Wendy," a polite, computerized voice chirped. "What will we be working on today?"

"Well, I'm interested in using this coaching thing to make myself more successful," Wendy said. It felt awkward to be conversing with the computer, but she reminded herself it was something she'd need to get used to sooner or later.

"Wonderful," the voice said. "Let us begin with your **Topic**. What do you most want to accomplish?"

"That's the tough part," Wendy said. "I feel like there's tons of stuff I need to accomplish. I'm just not sure where to begin!"

"Take your time," the computer chirped. "Let us address your concerns one at a time. How would you describe your ultimate goal in the broadest sense?"

Wendy took a moment to process this. Well, that would certainly make things easier. She tried to decide which of her troubles deserved the most attention—fundamentally, her woes seemed to all stem from the gap between herself and her team.

"I don't know," Wendy said. "I mean, I've got an idea, but it seems too big, too broad—I have no idea how I'd begin."

"Don't worry, Wendy," the coach said. "Right now, big and broad is exactly what you want! Remember, you'll have plenty of time to figure out how to solve it during the other steps."

"Where should I start, though?" Wendy asked.

"Well, let's try categorizing the issues," the coach said. "Try to think of an issue that's most prominent in your mind right now. Does it have to do with **People**, your **Process**, or **Safety**?"

Wendy took a moment to think about it. She reflected back on why she was struggling.

"People," she said.

"All right," the coach continued. "Let's work from there. What caused the issue, or better yet, what do you think you need to work on in order to prevent it from coming up again in the future? If it's a people issue, you might find it helpful to think about communication and your overall team dynamic."

"Hmm, that makes sense," Wendy said. "I think I can work with that."

She turned to the worksheet:

RESULTS-BASED COACHING MODEL

Action Planning Template – Wendy

TOPIC	WHAT ARE WE GOING TO BE WORKING ON?
	WHAT PROBLEM DO YOU NEED TO SOLVE?
	TEAM COHESIVENESS

CURRENT REALITY	WHAT IS WORKING WELL?	WHAT NEEDS IMPROVEMENT?

VISION	WHAT DOES IT NEED TO BE / LOOK LIKE?

SUCCESS	WHAT DOES SUCCESS LOOK LIKE?
	HOW DO YOU KNOW YOU HAVE GOTTEN THE RESULT YOU WANT?

ACTION	WHAT ARE YOU GOING TO DO?	WITH WHOM?	WHEN?

OBSTACLES	WHAT COULD GET IN THE WAY?	HOW WILL YOU OVERCOME IT?

UNDERSTANDING YOUR CURRENT REALITY

Making Progress

"Huh, that was pretty easy after all," Wendy said. "Thanks, Virtual Coach!"

"Of course," the Virtual Coach said. "Feel free to ask more questions when you need to—I will be here when you need help."

With the Virtual Coach's advice, coming up with an appropriate **Topic** had taken only a few moments for her. After all, the problem was staring her in the face.

Thinking of her situation, Wendy felt the frustration and irritation welling up again. Why was leading a sales team proving to be so difficult? It wasn't fair! She began to wonder if even something as promising as **Coaching** could help her improve.

"All right, I need to calm down," she said to herself, talking a deep breath. "Maybe some music would help." She put on her favorite radio station, turned the volume down to an ambient level, and glanced over the next section of the worksheet.

"**Current Reality**, huh?" she said. "Let's see, first is—what's not working well."

Well, that part was certainly easy! Wendy could think of a million things that weren't going well. The hard part would be narrowing it down to something she could work with!

"Okay, can't let myself get discouraged," she said. "Let's move on to the next one—what is working well. Hmm?"

She sat back for a moment, thinking. This would take some thought, she realized. On the bright side, she knew that the team consisted of hard workers with the same goal in mind. Personality conflicts in a group are natural – especially in a group of WOMEN!

The Here and Now

Before you can properly tackle any problem, big or small, you have to understand what you're getting into. In our coaching model, we call this taking stock of your **Current Reality**.

Start by asking yourself any number of basic questions about the situation. What is the issue at hand? How do you hope to improve? Why are you in the current situation—what obstacles are preventing improvement? Who is actively involved in this process? How do they feel about the situation? Some of these questions you might know the answer to right away, while others could go unanswered for a good while. That's perfectly okay at this stage—right now you're just brainstorming to get the fullest possible sense of where you are and what you're facing.

You're free to address whatever questions or concerns you like at this point. If you think it will be helpful, don't hesitate to include it! That said, using our coaching template, you'll probably find it useful to cover these important bases:

- **WHAT ARE WE GOING TO BE WORKING ON? WRITE ANY QUESTIONS AND ANSWERS IN THE "TOPIC" FIELD.** It's a simple step, but it will prove effective at keeping your thoughts focused and your actions on track throughout the process to come. What is the core concern you plan to address using coaching? This can start out as a broad or vague idea ("My business isn't making enough money," for example), but as you brainstorm, see if you can use the information you have to make it more specific ("My business isn't attracting as many new customers as it was last year"). The more focused your topic is, the easier it'll be to come up with an effective solution.

- **WHAT IS WORKING WELL? FILL IN THE LEFT HALF OF "CURRENT REALITY."** Even if you feel like things just aren't going right anywhere, take some time to think about what you and your business are doing well, big or small. Not only will this boost your confidence, but it will also help point out behaviors and trends that you can emphasize to promote growth and success.

- **WHAT NEEDS IMPROVEMENT? FILL IN THE RIGHT HALF OF "CURRENT REALITY."** Think of realistic goals for the near future, and again, be specific, if possible. If at this point you can come up with potential solutions, that's great, feel free to include it—at the very least, though, identify what needs to improve, even if you can't yet decide how to do it. Be honest, but avoid criticism or casting blame on individuals. Remember, a major part of being accountable is taking responsibility as a team!

Better Brainstorming Tips

Are you having trouble coming up with those bullet points? Here are a few questions you might try asking to find that spark of inspiration.

- **WHAT IS THE OPPORTUNITY HERE?** What is something you can currently take advantage of? Where do you have room to grow, or what sets you apart from someone else in your field? Besides using this as food for thought for thinking of new strengths, you can also ask the question to build from one to another, or from a strength to an improvement area. Okay, your business is really great at this particular task; now how can you use that to emphasize other strengths, or cover for a weakness elsewhere?

- **WHAT ARE THE DRIVERS?** What do you see as your primary motivator? This in itself can be a strength, or possibly even an issue to work on in the future. This is true whether the driver in question is a "carrot" or a "stick," so to speak—a desire for great rewards and satisfaction can be a very powerful motivator, and so can a strong will to avoid a particular bad outcome, but both can easily lead to undue stress if unchecked.

- **WHAT ARE THE BARRIERS?** If you had to name just one thing, what is preventing you from achieving your goal? Furthermore, what might become a bigger obstruction in the future? As we'll cover later on in the **Obstacles** chapter, we feel that no barrier is insurmountable, especially if you anticipate it and come up with a workaround early on.

The Here and Now, Continued

"I think I need help again, Virtual Coach," Wendy said.

"Current step: **Current Reality**," the coach beeped. "Now's the time to brainstorm freely! Just get all of your thoughts on the worksheet—what's working well, and what isn't?"

"I suppose that's easy enough," Wendy said. "How much should I write, though?"

"As much as you want," the coach replied. "The more, the better! I recommend at least trying to balance the 'works well' and 'needs improvement' columns, but besides that, there are no restrictions whatsoever."

"Hmm," Wendy said, sizing up the worksheet. "Still, there's not a whole lot of space to write much, is there?"

"Now, Wendy, you know that's not true," the coach said. "You're using an electronic document, so you can make the space as big as you need!"

"Oh yeah, you're right," Wendy said, feeling more than a little sheepish. She started putting down bullet points in the boxes, switching back and forth:

RESULTS-BASED COACHING MODEL

Action Planning Template – Wendy

TOPIC	WHAT ARE WE GOING TO BE WORKING ON? WHAT PROBLEM DO YOU NEED TO SOLVE?
	TEAM COHESIVENESS

CURRENT REALITY	WHAT IS WORKING WELL?	WHAT NEEDS IMPROVEMENT?
	COMMON GOAL HARD WORKERS TRUST IN OUR COMPANY, PRODUCT	COMMUNICATION WHAT MOTIVATES THEM/MAKES THEM FEEL LIKE THEY DO? PERSONALITY CONFLICTS

VISION	WHAT DOES IT NEED TO BE / LOOK LIKE?

SUCCESS	WHAT DOES SUCCESS LOOK LIKE? HOW DO YOU KNOW YOU HAVE GOTTEN THE RESULT YOU WANT?

ACTION	WHAT ARE YOU GOING TO DO?	WITH WHOM?	WHEN?

OBSTACLES	WHAT COULD GET IN THE WAY?	HOW WILL YOU OVERCOME IT?

CREATE YOUR VISION

In the Future, There Will Be Success

Wendy finished typing, and glanced over her work so far. Already a third of the way done and she managed to keep her columns balanced. Remarkable! This gave her a new sense of confidence—success was that much closer within her reach.

"We make a great team, don't we, Virtual Coach?" Wendy asked.

"We sure do, Wendy," the coach said. "I'll be here when you next need me!"

This was working – it was really working! Wendy was convinced that her team was going to work as a well oiled machine sooner rather than later. Really taking the time to analyze the team's strengths as well as its shortfalls had been beneficial, and Wendy was sure to include herself in the analysis; she wasn't exempt from the analysis just because she was the leader. She knew that she, herself, had things to work on. This certainly wasn't as easy as the training video implied, but Wendy was determined to succeed.

Wendy had hung her vision boards in her home office. She wanted to make sure that they were visible to her at all times. They also gave her some encouragement when she was struggling or feeling down. How fitting that the next empty box on the worksheet was **Vision**.

An Optimistic Vision

Our next step involves constructing a **Vision** of your ideal coaching outcome. Of course, you don't have to literally draw a picture, but if it helps,
by all means, don't hold back!

Whatever medium you choose to use, your goal at this stage is
to get a sense of your "finish line," so to speak. Having filled in your
Topic and **Current Reality**, you should already have a fairly good idea
of what your ultimate goal is, and this step will draw upon very similar
concerns.

What distinguishes this step from the others, though, is the intended
level of focus. During the **Topic** stage, we encouraged you to pull back
and come up with something more broad or general; now's the time to
delve more into specifics. Picture your ideal end result, such as a more
profitable business, or a healthier social atmosphere in the workplace,
and zoom in on the details. What, specifically, makes your business profitable, and what kind of little practices and tweaks keep it that way?
How do employee interactions play out now that any tension has been
dispelled, and what role do you play in all of it? Basically, why did your
Vision come true, and what makes it different from your **Current Reality**,
besides having achieved your goal?

These are some heavy questions, to be sure, and they won't necessarily be easy to come up with answers for. Fortunately, by following
along up to this point, we've given you the tools you need to get started.
If you're having trouble with the little details, go back to **Current Reality**
and reflect on what you wrote there. Think about the individual points
on the "working well" side. How can you emphasize or encourage that
strength, and/or expand its presence, and what will the visible result be
once you've done that? Also zoom in on the points you filled in on the
"improvement" side, one at a time. What sort of measures could you take
to alleviate that particular issue, and what would your overall business
procedure look like if those measures became permanent?

The overall coaching process involves quite a bit of big-picture thinking throughout, but now is definitely the prime time to start thinking about it as a forward-moving process. If we take a cue from Wendy's vision boards and give the visioning process a distinct shape, it would look something like the following:

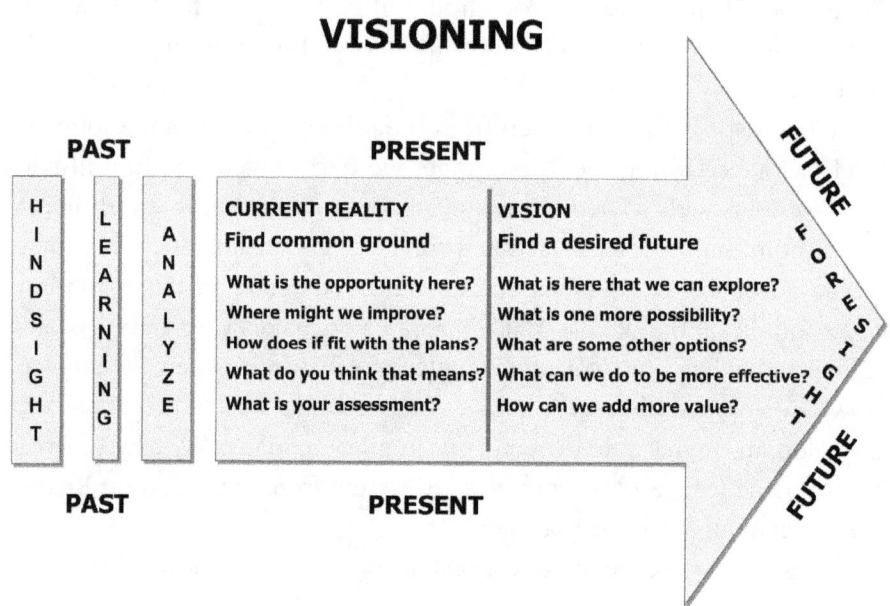

VISIONING

PAST   **PRESENT**   **FUTURE FOR ESIGHT**

HINDSIGHT	LEARNING	ANALYZE	CURRENT REALITY	VISION
			Find common ground	Find a desired future
			What is the opportunity here?	What is here that we can explore?
			Where might we improve?	What is one more possibility?
			How does if fit with the plans?	What are some other options?
			What do you think that means?	What can we do to be more effective?
			What is your assessment?	How can we add more value?

PAST   **PRESENT**   **FUTURE**

Essentially, by following the process in order thus far, we've been carrying out a natural progression through time, just like in the chart above: we start with the past, examine the present, and ultimately arrive at the future. Whatever issues or concerns led you to try out this coaching model were products of your business' past and present, and analyzing your **Current Reality** encouraged you to take stock of these phases. In a nutshell, we asked: where are you now (present), and what led you to this point (past)? When you determined your **Topic**, you caught a brief glimpse of the future; now, starting with **Vision**, that's where we'll keep most of our focus from here on out. We'll look at the present, as well, since you'll need to draw upon your business' current resources, but the aim, of course, will be building a better future.

Better Brainstorming Tips, Continued

If you're feeling overwhelmed by all of this abstract brainstorming, never fear! Try asking a few of these questions to de-cloud your crystal ball.

- **WHAT CAN WE EXPLORE?** At this stage in the brainstorming process, try not to be too concerned about grounding yourself in any set of expectations. If you can imagine it, you can do it! No idea is too radical—mentally follow it into your future **Vision**, and see where it might take you.

- **WHAT IS ONE MORE POSSIBILITY?** Don't feel compelled to restrict yourself to just one **Vision**. The future is, by its very nature, unpredictable, and any number of factors could contribute to all sorts of different outcomes. Imagine a different result—it could be better, worse, or simply different—and make preparations for that one, too. If things happen to lead to that outcome instead, you won't be caught off guard, and in any case, you'll have a good backup plan prepared if need be.

- **HOW CAN WE ADD MORE VALUE?** While Wendy's story is meant to emphasize the value of coaching as a one-on-one process, don't hesitate to bring in your teammates if they're willing to contribute. What are their **Visions**, and how are the similar or different compared to yours? Remember, a coach who listens to his or her players has a much stronger team for it!

In the Future, There Will Be Success, Continued

"I just don't see it coming full circle yet," Wendy sighed, glancing back at her vision boards.

"Come now, Wendy," the virtual coach beeped. "Clearly, you have a clear sense of what your ideal **Vision** looks like! You just need to find a way to express it in a practical sense."

"But I'm having trouble finding the right words to describe it," Wendy said.

"No one said it needed to be described in words; even just the picture could be enough, if it makes sense to you," the coach replied. "You just

31

need to ground your **Vision** in something concrete that you can accurately describe. More specificity is better, as it'll make it all the easier to recognize when that **Vision** becomes **Reality**!"

"Well, that makes sense," Wendy said. "I think I've got it now—I created these vision boards before I even knew about the program. I was ahead of the game and didn't even realize it until now!"

"Do whatever makes the most sense to you," the coach said.

Glancing back and forth between her vision boards and the worksheet, Wendy brainstormed ways to describe it:

RESULTS-BASED COACHING MODEL

Action Planning Template - Wendy

TOPIC	WHAT ARE WE GOING TO BE WORKING ON?
	WHAT PROBLEM DO YOU NEED TO SOLVE?
	TEAM COHESIVENESS

CURRENT REALITY	WHAT IS WORKING WELL?	WHAT NEEDS IMPROVEMENT?
	COMMON GOAL	COMMUNICATION
	HARD WORKERS	WHAT MOTIVATES THEM/MAKES THEM FEEL LIKE THEY DO?
	TRUST IN OUR COMPANY, PRODUCT	PERSONALITY CONFLICTS

VISION	WHAT DOES IT NEED TO BE / LOOK LIKE?
	I WANT TO BE THE LEADER THAT I KNOW I CAN BE
	RESPECT FOR ONE ANOTHER AS INDIVIDUALS AND AS A TEAM
	WORKING AS ONE UNIT TOWARD THE COMMON GOAL
	MAINTAIN PROFESSIONALISM AND REPRESENT OUR COMPANY WELL

SUCCESS	WHAT DOES SUCCESS LOOK LIKE?
	HOW DO YOU KNOW YOU HAVE GOTTEN THE RESULT YOU WANT?

ACTION	WHAT ARE YOU GOING TO DO?	WITH WHOM?	WHEN?

OBSTACLES	WHAT COULD GET IN THE WAY?	HOW WILL YOU OVERCOME IT?

ACHIEVING SUCCESS

One Giant Leap

Wendy's **Vision** was optimistic, but she was a believer in herself and she was a believer in her team. The team members may not all see the same vision just yet, but Wendy knew that she was on the road to success! Wendy had always considered herself an optimist and she was not about to possess a pessimistic attitude now.

"Halfway there already!" Wendy said. "Sorry to keep you up so late, Virtual Coach."

"Don't worry, Wendy," the coach said. "I'm a computer program, and don't need to sleep. You should take a break every now and then, though!"

Wendy had to admit that it seemed like an attractive proposal. She checked the clock. It had gotten very late, but she was afraid that sleep would have to wait. Wendy felt like she was really on to something and she knew that if she went to bed she wouldn't sleep anyway. Her mind was racing with possibilities and she couldn't turn her mind off as quickly as her body! She would only lay awake thinking if she went to bed now. Besides, she had only three more topics to cover!

A Vision of Success

Ready to do some time traveling? Think back on the arrow chart we introduced in the previous chapter. For this step, we'll maintain our strong focus on the future.

First of all, you need to consider what your eventual **Success** looks like. How will you know for sure when you've achieved the goal you set up in your **Topic**? What specific indicators should you look for? Looking back on your **Current Reality** will help a great deal here. When you've noticeably cleared up one of the bullet points on the "room for improvement" side, you'll know you're that much closer to your goal. When you've cleared up all of them, chances are that means it's time to bask in your achievement and whip up a new worksheet!

This part of the step shares a lot in common with the previous one, **Vision**. After you've become comfortable with the coaching process and try it again in the future, you may even prefer to do the two parts simultaneously, as they go hand-in-hand. Figuring out your **Success** involves measurement of the steps to reach your established **Vision**.

Of course, it certainly won't hurt to do both steps in quick succession, and play them off of one another. Think critically about the future you want to fulfill, and above all, stay optimistic—following the steps to come, you'll be able to make it a reality!

One Giant Leap, Continued

After pouring herself a cup of hot tea, Wendy sat back down at the computer.

"How is your progress on the worksheet?" the coach asked. "Ah, I see you're already on the **Success** section!"

"Yes, I am moving right along," Wendy said. "It seems kind of strange, though. It says I'm supposed to think about how I know when I've gotten the right result—didn't I just do that?"

"You're right, the two steps are quite similar," the coach said. "What sets them apart is measurement."

"Measurement?" Wendy echoed. "What do you mean?"

"Well, when you did the **Vision** step, you were just focusing on one point in the future, speculating about what it would look like," the coach replied. "For this step, though, try to imagine yourself working your way up to that. What will it take to get there, and how will you be able to tell that you're making progress? That's where measurement will come in."

"Hmm," Wendy mused. "I think I can see what you mean."

"Take your time, and feel free to ask questions if you're stuck," the coach said. "I'll walk you through it, so don't worry—for now, just put down whatever comes to mind."

"OK, I'll try," Wendy said.

RESULTS-BASED COACHING MODEL

Action Planning Template – Wendy

TOPIC	WHAT ARE WE GOING TO BE WORKING ON? WHAT PROBLEM DO YOU NEED TO SOLVE?
	TEAM COHESIVENESS

	WHAT IS WORKING WELL?	WHAT NEEDS IMPROVEMENT?
CURRENT REALITY	COMMON GOAL HARD WORKERS TRUST IN OUR COMPANY, PRODUCT	COMMUNICATION WHAT MOTIVATES THEM/MAKES THEM FEEL LIKE THEY DO? PERSONALITY CONFLICTS

VISION	WHAT DOES IT NEED TO BE / LOOK LIKE?
	I WANT TO BE THE LEADER I KNOW I CAN BE RESPECT FOR ONE ANOTHER AS INDIVIDUALS AND AS A TEAM WORKING AS ONE UNIT TOWARD THE COMMON GOAL MAINTAINING PROFESSIONALISM AND REPRESENTING OUR COMPANY WELL

SUCCESS	WHAT DOES SUCCESS LOOK LIKE? HOW DO YOU KNOW YOU HAVE GOTTEN THE RESULT YOU WANT?
	SUCCESS: WHEN MY TEAM IS WORKING TOGETHER, POSITIVELY REPRESENTING THE COMPANY/PRODUCT THAT WE BELIEVE IN, AND EARNING A COMFORTABLE LIVING ALL WHILE ENJOYING TIME WITH OUR FAMILIES AND FRIENDS. WHEN MY TEAM CAN BE SUCCESSFUL WITH OR WITHOUT ME. WHEN MY TEAM MEMBERS BEGIN TO RECRUIT OTHER TEAM MEMBERS TO WORK UNDER THEIR GUIDANCE. WHEN THE COMPANY THAT WE REPRESENT ACKNOWLEDGES US FOR OUR EFFORTS. ULTIMATELY, WHEN WE CAN BE THE SPOUSE AND PARENTS OUR FAMILY NEEDS WHILE EARNING AN INCOME.

	WHAT ARE YOU GOING TO DO?	WITH WHOM?	WHEN?
ACTION			

	WHAT COULD GET IN THE WAY?	HOW WILL YOU OVERCOME IT?
OBSTACLES		

TIME FOR ACTION

A Girl's Got to Do What a Girl's Got to Do

"So, that's how you do the **Success** step," the virtual coach said. "Does that make sense?"

"Yeah, I think so," Wendy said. "Thanks, Virtual Coach! I don't know how I'd get through any of this without your help."

"Of course, Wendy," the coach said. "That's what I was programmed for! Feel free to call for me if you have further questions."

At the moment, Wendy's motivation levels were at an all-time high. This worksheet was really putting Wendy's ideas into perspective. Breaking everything down step-by-step was a life saver. She had felt so overwhelmed just hours before and now she was two-thirds of the way to having a complete action plan! She knew that this template was exactly what she had needed. She had lost focus and had almost given up on her dream...now she felt as if it was all within her reach once again. Now, she just had to come up with a way to make this **Success** a reality.

"Let's see—I've got to come up with **Actions**," Wendy said. Wendy knew that the **Actions** portion may be tough because the success was riding on everyone in the team, not just her. She knew that she was going to have to develop actions that everyone on the team would be willing to do.

Wendy, being the optimist, began planning out her strategy. First, everyone would have to re-dedicate themselves to this new plan. If they weren't willing to work as a team and for the betterment of the team, they would have to be removed from the team. Only team players from here on out! This was a hard reality, and Wendy never liked to be "the bad guy" but their success was riding on it. All for one and one for all!

Now's the Time to Take Action (or Plan It Out, Anyway)!

Hopefully, in the midst of all the brainstorming we've been doing about your business' present and future, you spent some time focusing on how the strengths in your **Current Reality** could be used to achieve **Success**. If so, great! This step will simply expand on all of that, and will be very easy to get started on. Even if you haven't yet had the chance to think about such topics, though, we'll still be building off the work you've done so far, so you're already well on your way!

This is it, the critical step you've been waiting for: now is the time for **Action**! It may be a bit of a misnomer, as you won't yet be actually executing any of the plans you write here—that will come a little later, once the worksheet is all filled out—but this will directly lead to the exciting step of using all of your planning and hard work to score a big payoff. Keep it up, you're doing great so far and you're almost there!

Think of this section like a road map, or perhaps a movie script. Each **Action** you plan to take will be set up like a scene or a plot point, and you'll ask yourself some appropriate accompanying questions. First of all, what are you going to do? Second, with whom are you going to do it? Third, when will this take place?

This will cover the important basics, but if you want to keep going, you may want to give yourself even more detailed instructions, using extra room, the back of the worksheet, or another piece of paper. For instance, where will you be when you carry this out? Just as an example, let's say you plan to have a gentle, constructive talk with a teammate about a negative attitude on the job—typically, doing it in private would be the most tactful option, but you'd want to avoid framing it in a way that seems like intimidation or a power play (perhaps you'd want to pull them aside or contact them later, rather than addressing them at a team meeting). Another good question: why will you take this particular step? Chances are answering this question will involve nearly pure review, but it can be a helpful tool for keeping track of how all the little pieces will fall into place as you strive towards your goal.

At this point, you're free to allow yourself plenty of wiggle room, and can edit any or all aspects of a task on the fly, should a good reason for it come up. Just be sure that you're happy with it when you finish the worksheet, because it will be important to faithfully stick to your plans once it's time to actually carry them out! If you like, you can keep a list of your actions in a notebook or other small, separate location, and treat it like a to-do list, checking each one off as they're completed, and perhaps even marking them in a different way if they directly led to an achieved goal. Sometimes little bursts of satisfaction like these are all you need to keep going forward!

The Resourceful Businessperson

The **Action** step has a lot to do with *what* you're going to do, naturally, but it's also critical to consider *how* you'll accomplish it. We already briefly mentioned drawing on the strengths listed in your **Current Reality**, and this section will be fairly similar. In order to get you closer to your goal, we're going to take stock of your available **Resources**.

So, what can count as a **Resource**? For the purpose of our coaching model, we're defining this concept as literally anything your business has that may specifically help you achieve your goal. These can be particular people, places, or things; they can even be more abstract concepts, such as skills, opportunities, or your business' history and reputation. A good **Resource's** function may be relatively obvious—let's say, for example, money—or it can be more open to interpretation, if it's something like, for instance, time.

Previously, we spent time talking about how the little defining details of your business could potentially be improved, as well as how you might be able to draw out new strengths as you carry out the coaching process. At the moment, though, we're going to focus almost exclusively on the present. We want to come up with a list of strengths, possessions, and other beneficial traits that your business has *right now* that can contribute to **Actions** leading to your **Success**. Don't sell yourself short, either—your business is sure to have, at the very least, a few solid **Resources** that are within your grasp and, regardless of how they're being used now, can be leveraged into major growth and improvement. If you struggled earlier to fill in the "what works" section of **Current Reality**, now's the time to revisit the topic and challenge yourself. Don't let yourself move on until you've filled in that whole box!

As you brainstorm about your current **Resources**, you may find it helpful to consider them in relation to the various minor improvements and sub-goals you've come up with so far, as opposed to just the big goal in your **Topic**. It may be difficult to connect a given strength to the big-picture **Success** you've outlined, but if you use it to fix a smaller issue, and that leads you closer to your ideal outcome, that certainly counts for a lot! Of course, **Resources** can be flexible, as well—some, like money and time, have a bit more scarcity than others, but a **Resource** like a motivated, dependable person on your team can, if encouraged, become a constant source of overall growth and success!

This task has many practical applications, as you'll likely be able to better appreciate and make use of your **Resources** on your way to your goal, but we definitely can't rule out the motivational side of it. Remember: even in the gloomiest of circumstances, you can always count on a **Resource** to help lift you up! The trick, of course, is looking for and finding it. Just keep on brainstorming, bring in teammates for input if you're stuck (or if you're not—either way they can be very helpful), and don't stop until you've got them cornered on the page!

Going for Goals the "SMART" Way
As you're setting up your **Action** plans and tying them into the various goals you aim to fulfill, there are a few tips you'll want to keep in mind. To sum it up in one word, you'll want to be "SMART." Why the all-caps, you ask? Why, it's a handy acrostic, of course!

- SPECIFIC

- MEASURABLE

- ACTIONABLE

- RELEVANT

- TIMELY

All are positive, desirable qualities and buzzwords, to be sure. Naturally, though, we won't just leave you hanging with that! Let's go over each of our choices, and why we felt it was important to single them out.

- **SPECIFIC.** You may remember our advice from a few chapters back on tying your strengths and **Resources** to smaller, more specific goals, rather than the big, broad one from your **Topic**. That's very relevant here, too! Assuming your **Topic** is appropriately open-ended, it's unreasonable to expect to be able to take care of it with any single, all-encompassing action. The purpose of this section, and several that preceded it, is to break that big goal down into a variety of smaller projects, and work your way to success one manageable piece at a time. You should end up with a healthy variety of **Actions** planned out, and each one should ideally focus on contributing to a specific, small sub-goal.

- **MEASURABLE.** A given **Action** may be helpful, but it'll be tough to feel any sense of satisfaction if it's not clear how it helped you, or if you don't have a way of knowing if it was even helpful in the first place. Think back on the first part of the **Success** phase, when you thought about what particular markers would indicate that you'd achieved your big goal. We'll do something similar here, asking ourselves the question: will this **Action** produce accurate data, and will we be able to identify and/or measure it?

- **ACTIONABLE.** This one's pretty simple: will you be able to carry out the **Action**? To expand on that a bit, you'll want to create a task that is easy to understand in every category, and that you (and any other active participants) feel confident and comfortable about. The last thing you want is to arrive at the moment for an **Action** only to find that you don't remember everything you intended to do or why you intended to do it, or worse, forget about it entirely and miss the intended time. Being clear and detailed in your instructions will help you plenty down the line, and will also ensure that the teammates working on it with you are able to fulfill your expectations.

- **RELEVANT.** This may seem obvious, but it can be surprisingly easy to get overly caught up in the freedom of brainstorming, and wind up with a lot of ambitious-sounding plans that, in practice, probably won't address the goals at hand. Stay grounded in your **Topic** and your sub-goals, and try to stick to **Actions** that have a clear connection to them and/or are likely to produce useful results and information.

- **TIMELY.** A well-planned **Action** may be a splendid idea, but still needs to be executed at the right time for the best results. When you're planning your timetable and filling in the "when" box, think about how the tasks should be logically ordered, as well as how they might best capitalize on predicted time-sensitive trends or opportunities. More advanced users may even want to plan a series of timed actions as a "chain reaction" of sorts—one task will produce data that will contribute to the success of a subsequent item, which can in turn lead to the next one, and so on.

Remember to stay SMART, and you'll be well on your way to turning your to-do list into a *can*-do list!

As always, collaboration with teammates is a helpful part of the coaching process, but during this step, keep in mind that it's especially crucial, since many of your planned **Actions** will involve one or more of them. If you plan on having a particular teammate actively participate in a task, make sure you include them in the planning process! It'll be hard for someone else to be enthusiastic about a growth objective that's sprung on them without any input or consent.

Overall, as you carry out this step, be sure to carefully consider all of the information you've brainstormed about up to this point, and take all the time you need to develop realistic **Action** plans. You'll be carrying these plans out and actively engaging with your business' coaching-fueled growth in the very near future—stay positive, stay focused, and work your way towards success!

A Girl's Got to Do What a Girl's Got to Do, Continued

"This seems like a really hard part, coach," Wendy said. "I mean, this is really the most important step, isn't it? This will decide whether or not the whole thing succeeds down the line!"

"It is indeed important," the coach agreed. "However, try not to get *too* caught up in thinking about the 'what-ifs.' Remember, any idea is potentially worth considering—you just have to be willing to brainstorm it out!"

"Well, all right, I can do that," Wendy said. "How should I get started, though?"

"Just treat it like a to-do list," the coach suggested. "Think about your goals and desires from the previous steps, and think about how you'd go about fulfilling them. Start with the short term and work your way up to the long term—once you get started, I think you'll find it much easier to keep going from there."

"That sounds like a good idea," Wendy said. "All right, I'll give it a shot! Let's see what I can come up with."

Wendy took the coach's advice, and started small, thinking about what she'd need to do immediately. With this in mind, she started writing:

RESULTS-BASED COACHING MODEL

Action Planning Template – Wendy

TOPIC	WHAT ARE WE GOING TO BE WORKING ON? WHAT PROBLEM DO YOU NEED TO SOLVE?
	TEAM COHESIVENESS

CURRENT REALITY	WHAT IS WORKING WELL?	WHAT NEEDS IMPROVEMENT?
	COMMON GOAL	COMMUNICATION
	HARD WORKERS	WHAT MOTIVATES THEM/MAKES THEM FEEL LIKE THEY DO?
	TRUST IN OUR COMPANY/PRODUCT	PERSONALITY CONFLICTS

VISION	WHAT DOES IT NEED TO BE / LOOK LIKE?
	I WANT TO BE THE LEADER I KNOW I CAN BE
	RESPECT FOR ONE ANOTHER AS INDIVIDUALS AND AS A TEAM
	WORKING AS ONE UNIT TOWARD THE COMMON GOAL
	MAINTAINING PROFESSIONALISM AND REPRESENTING OUR COMPANY WELL

SUCCESS	WHAT DOES SUCCESS LOOK LIKE? HOW DO YOU KNOW YOU HAVE GOTTEN THE RESULT YOU WANT?
	SUCCESS: WHEN MY TEAM IS WORKING TOGETHER, POSITIVELY REPRESENTING THE COMPANY/PRODUCT THAT WE BELIEVE IN, AND EARNING A COMFORTABLE LIVING ALL WHILE ENJOYING TIME WITH OUR FAMILIES AND FRIENDS.
	WHEN MY TEAM CAN BE SUCCESSFUL WITH OR WITHOUT ME.
	WHEN MY TEAM MEMBERS BEGIN TO RECRUIT OTHER TEAM MEMBERS TO WORK UNDER THEIR GUIDANCE.
	WHEN THE COMPANY THAT WE REPRESENT ACKNOWLEDGES US FOR OUR EFFORTS.
	ULTIMATELY, WHEN WE CAN BE THE SPOUSE AND PARENTS OUR FAMILY NEEDS WHILE EARNING AN INCOME.

ACTION	WHAT ARE YOU GOING TO DO?	WITH WHOM?	WHEN?
	VISIT COMPANY WEBSITE FOR UPDATED SUCCESS STORIES	MYSELF	TOMORROW
	CALL A TEAM MEETING; INVITE OPINIONS AND INPUT	WHOLE TEAM	THURSDAY
	MEET WITH EACH TEAM MEMBER TO DETERMINE LEVEL OF INTEREST	TEAM MEMBERS	THIS WEEKEND
	MEET WITH NEW FOUNDATION TEAM; DISCUSS TEAM GOALS, GROWTH, SUCCESS	WHOLE TEAM	NEXT WEEK
	BOOST TEAM MORALE BY HOSTING A TEAM BONDING WEEKEND	WHOLE TEAM	NEXT WEEKEND

OBSTACLES	WHAT COULD GET IN THE WAY?	HOW WILL YOU OVERCOME IT?

VIII

OVERCOMING POTENTIAL OBSTACLES

Putting it All Into Action

Wendy felt she'd put together a pretty good **Action** list, if she did say so herself. Well, she figured she'd earned at least that much.

"I've put together a pretty good **Action** list," she said so to herself.

"Yes, I'd say you have," the virtual coach observed. "Feel free to add to it in the future, but for now, it looks like you've got a solid plan about what to do next."

"Yeah, I think so," Wendy said. "I feel like I'm in good shape for now, but I'll give you a call if anything comes up. Thanks, Virtual Coach!"

The coach's avatar smiled, nodded, and faded into the background. Wendy was proud of herself. She saw what was standing between her and success and she was creating the map to get her to her end result. She knew that it wouldn't be easy and that writing everything down was the easy part. She never liked being the bearer of bad news and she certainly didn't want to kick someone off the team – but she knew that she may have to do just that. It certainly wasn't anything personal, just part of the process.

As Wendy finished her cup of hot tea she looked back at the worksheet, "Let's see here. **Obstacles?**" Wendy frowned at the sight of that word. Amidst all the motivation momentum and positive reinforcement, she'd completely neglected to consider that she might still face problems in her quest. What a downer!

Wendy felt as if the wind had been knocked out of her sails. All of this positive talk and now she was going to have to focus on obstacles that may stand in the way of her success? Shaking the negativity from her head, she forged on because she knew that she had already overcome the biggest obstacle by seeking help when she realized that her team was in trouble.

Anticipate (Then Avoid) Obstacles

First of all, congratulations on making it this far! You've done a lot of hard work and have brainstormed, brainstormed, and then brainstormed some more for good measure. You're almost there—just one more step to go, and then your journey to business growth can truly begin!

Every step of the way, we've offered plenty of motivational spirit and aimed to foster a can-do attitude. Optimism, after all, will carry you quite a long way. With that said, it may at first seem a bit out-of-place for us to pick this moment to discuss potential **Obstacles**. Why would we bring you crashing down like that?

Not only is it vital that we cover such a topic in the first place, but we also stand by the notion that right now, at this very moment, is the best possible time to talk about **Obstacles**. So far, you've spent all this time planning for future **Success**, drawing on the tools and abilities you currently have at your disposal to work towards it. Now, we're going to take that thinking and apply it to the near future—not the future in which your **Vision** has come true, but in the time between now and then, when any number of unknown factors could come into play. It's far better to think realistically about those now than to take a big hit to your business' momentum being caught by surprise later on.

Despite appearances, this section has the potential to be a powerful positive motivator in itself. It may help to think of **Obstacles** not as possible causes of failure, but instead as new opportunities to call upon your **Resources** and planned **Actions**, whether you've already tapped into them or not. In fact, this section's location makes perfect sense following up the **Action** planning phase—basically, you'll be doing the same thing you did in the previous chapter, but instead of setting tasks to address present goals and issues, you'll pull in a good amount of brainstorming to take on hypothetical future concerns.

When you fill in this box, treat it pretty much the same way you did the **Action** field. Think of a particular obstacle or issue, then come up with an appropriate countermeasure or two. In effect, you're setting new sub-goals (and at the same time, your intended means of fulfilling them) well before they come into relevance, so that you'll be completely ready to face them if and when the time comes.

Better Brainstorming Tips

Of course, as we've stated numerous times before, predicting the future is no easy task. We wouldn't expect you to achieve 100% accuracy in this section, and neither should you. Still, there are a few tips you can keep in mind to get the most out of this phase of the worksheet.

- **BE A BIT BROAD.** In the **Action** step, we stressed the importance of being specific about your plans, and for that section, as well as most of the ones preceding it, that still stands. Here, however, you're more likely to benefit from being a bit more vague, and coming up with **Obstacles** that could potentially encompass a variety of scenarios as opposed to one super-specific issue. Think of yourself here like a deep pass defender in a football game: naturally, before the play, he doesn't know exactly where the receiver will go, so he covers an area instead of a specific target. That way, he can cover anyone who enters that area, and won't be fooled by following just one man and finding out it was the wrong choice. By the same token, prepare yourself for a big-picture problem with many possible manifestations—you can even think of this section as coming up with potential future worksheet **Topics**, if you like.

- **DRAW UPON THE PRESENT.** If you're not comfortable spending too much time dwelling on complete unknowns, why not focus on what you do know? You already have a list of present concerns and goals in your **Current Reality** section.

What if one of these issues stuck around later on, or evolved somehow? Think also about your planned **Actions**. What if one of them doesn't get you the result you were hoping for, and the problem remains? What would be a good backup or secondary task to perform to try to fix it? If you're still having trouble, a somewhat heavy-handed approach is to revisit the **Vision** and **Success** fields. Picture a future **Vision** again, but instead of sticking to optimism, consider what the situation might look like if your plans go sour. Then work backwards from there. How did it get to that point? What problems, both including and in addition to the ones you face presently, were a contributing factor? In a similar vein, what might happen as a result if a given minor problem is left alone? Whatever you need to do to find inspiration and get a heavy brainstorm going is worth pursuing.

Putting it All Into Action, Continued

Wendy hovered over the program tab for a moment, considering whether she really needed help. Thinking she'd be better off safe than sorry, she clicked on it, bringing the Virtual Coach back into the foreground.

"Hello again, Wendy," the coach said. "I see you're almost finished! Do you need my assistance?"

"Possibly," Wendy said. "I think I've got the idea, but I just wanted to make sure I'm doing this right."

"All right," the coach said. "What do you have in mind?"

"So, this is the **Obstacles** step," Wendy said. "Basically, I'm just thinking of problems that might come up in the future, then coming up with ways to get around them, right?"

"You've got the right idea," the coach said. "Of course, I'd also recommend thinking about ways to prevent the **Obstacles** from coming up in the first place, if possible—they'd be much easier to deal with that way! Other than that, though, it sounds like you're thinking in exactly the right direction."

"Great," Wendy said. "Say, this is pretty similar to the **Action** step, isn't it?"

"Indeed it is," the coach replied. "You're doing something very similar—the only major difference is that, instead of addressing current concerns, you're dealing with possible future issues."

"I think I feel pretty good about this section going in, then," Wendy said. "Thanks, Virtual Coach! Again, you've been extremely helpful."

"My pleasure, Wendy," the coach said. "Call me if you need me!"

The coach faded away once more. Wendy turned to the worksheet and began to type:

RESULTS-BASED COACHING MODEL

Action Planning Template - Wendy

<table>
<tr><td rowspan="2">TOPIC</td><td colspan="2">WHAT ARE WE GOING TO BE WORKING ON?
WHAT PROBLEM DO YOU NEED TO SOLVE?</td></tr>
<tr><td colspan="2">TEAM COHESIVENESS</td></tr>
</table>

<table>
<tr><td rowspan="2">CURRENT REALITY</td><td>WHAT IS WORKING WELL?</td><td>WHAT NEEDS IMPROVEMENT?</td></tr>
<tr><td>COMMON GOAL
HARD WORKERS
TRUST IN OUR COMPANY/PRODUCT</td><td>COMMUNICATION
WHAT MOTIVATES THEM/MAKES THEM FEEL LIKE THEY DO?
PERSONALITY CONFLICTS</td></tr>
</table>

<table>
<tr><td rowspan="2">VISION</td><td>WHAT DOES IT NEED TO BE / LOOK LIKE?</td></tr>
<tr><td>I WANT TO BE THE LEADER I KNOW I CAN BE
RESPECT FOR ONE ANOTHER AS INDIVIDUALS AND AS A TEAM
WORKING AS ONE UNIT TOWARD THE COMMON GOAL
MAINTAINING PROFESSIONALISM AND REPRESENTING OUR COMPANY WELL</td></tr>
</table>

<table>
<tr><td rowspan="2">SUCCESS</td><td>WHAT DOES SUCCESS LOOK LIKE?
HOW DO YOU KNOW YOU HAVE GOTTEN THE RESULT YOU WANT?</td></tr>
<tr><td>SUCCESS: WHEN MY TEAM IS WORKING TOGETHER, POSITIVELY REPRESENTING THE COMPANY/PRODUCT THAT WE BELIEVE IN, AND EARNING A COMFORTABLE LIVING ALL WHILE ENJOYING TIME WITH OUR FAMILIES AND FRIENDS.

WHEN MY TEAM CAN BE SUCCESSFUL WITH OR WITHOUT ME.
WHEN MY TEAM MEMBERS BEGIN TO RECRUIT OTHER TEAM MEMBERS TO WORK UNDER THEIR GUIDANCE.
WHEN THE COMPANY THAT WE REPRESENT ACKNOWLEDGES US FOR OUR EFFORTS.
ULTIMATELY, WHEN WE CAN BE THE SPOUSE AND PARENTS OUR FAMILY NEEDS WHILE EARNING AN INCOME.</td></tr>
</table>

<table>
<tr><td rowspan="2">ACTION</td><td>WHAT ARE YOU GOING TO DO?</td><td>WITH WHOM?</td><td>WHEN?</td></tr>
<tr><td>VISIT COMPANY WEBSITE FOR UPDATED SUCCESS STORIES
CALL A TEAM MEETING; INVITE OPINIONS AND INPUT
MEET WITH EACH TEAM MEMBER TO DETERMINE LEVEL OF INTEREST
MEET WITH NEW FOUNDATION TEAM; DISCUSS TEAM GOALS, GROWTH, SUCCESS
BOOST TEAM MORALE BY HOSTING A TEAM BONDING WEEKEND</td><td>MYSELF
WHOLE TEAM
TEAM MEMBERS
WHOLE TEAM
WHOLE TEAM</td><td>TOMORROW
THURSDAY
THIS WEEKEND
NEXT WEEK
NEXT WEEKEND</td></tr>
</table>

<table>
<tr><td rowspan="2">OBSTACLES</td><td>WHAT COULD GET IN THE WAY?</td><td>HOW WILL YOU OVERCOME IT?</td></tr>
<tr><td>WEBSITE DOESN'T OFFER SUCCESS STORIES OF TEAM CONFLICT
TEAM MEMBERS SIT QUIETLY AND OFFER NO INPUT
THE ENTIRE TEAM QUITS BECAUSE OF LACK OF INTEREST
NEW FOUNDATION TEAM LACKS ENTHUSIASM AND DRIVE
WEEKEND IS A BUST BECAUSE OF SCHEDULING CONFLICTS</td><td>LOOK ELSEWHERE
STRESS THE IMPORTANCE OF OPEN LINES OF COMMUNICATION
RE-GROUP AND BEGIN BUILDING A NEW TEAM
REMAIN POSITIVE AND SHOW THEM THE POTENTIAL SUCCESS
THINK OF ACTIVITIES THAT DON'T TAKE AWAY FROM FAMILY TIME</td></tr>
</table>

MEASURING RESULTS

Better Team Morale

Wendy polished off the last of the entries on the worksheet. She was feeling a mix of emotions. She had created and filled out a great number of documents in her time. None, however, had given her the same sense of satisfaction upon completion as this simple worksheet.

"This is really something, coach," she said.

"Indeed it is, Wendy," the coach said. "I'm happy I was able to help. Do you have any further questions before I shut down?"

"No, I suppose not," Wendy said. "I'll sure be sad to see you go, though."

"Don't worry, Wendy," the coach said reassuringly. "I'll be here to help you for the next one, too! I look forward to seeing the results of your coaching plan in action."

"Yeah, me too," Wendy said. "In that case, I'll see you then!"

The coach waved goodbye, and the program closed. Wendy was anxious to get started as soon as she could, and see her plan in action. She checked the clock once more. Morning certainly loomed a lot closer, but it would still be quite a few hours before the sun came up. Before undergoing this "coaching" thing, she'd never felt such a strong sense of anticipation—all she wanted at the moment was to see a clear result come about from her actions, and she felt burdened by both the eagerness and the apprehension. She decided to try to get a few hours of sleep...but she knew that she wouldn't be able to sleep a wink.

Knowing When You've Succeeded

If you've been following along with the coaching process by filling in the worksheet as you go, feel free to step back and admire your handiwork. Look at how much work you've gotten done since you started! Way to go! It may be just a first step, but you've certainly experienced your first taste of coaching success.

At this point, we're effectively done with the worksheet—at least, we're done adding to it (for the most part—in some cases, such as if a particular plan definitely isn't working, you're naturally free to revisit the drawing board). Now would be the time to review what you've written and make any last-step adjustments. If you just recently thought of a great bullet point you missed, or a late section inspired you to edit an earlier one, this is as good an opportunity as any to make those changes. Also, now that you're no longer in pure, unfettered brainstorming mode, this is a good time to trim content that no longer seems appropriate, helpful, or effective, if there is any.

Once you come up with a finalized worksheet you can be happy with, you'll be ready to jump in and start carrying your plan out. Of course, this is just another step in the coaching process, and it's certainly an important one! Bear with us just a little longer, though, and we'll walk you through everything you'll need to keep in mind to pull off your plans without a hitch.

For starters, although you no longer need to edit the worksheet, you'll definitely want to refer to sections of it during this final phase. Here are the boxes that'll remain especially relevant post-planning:

- **ACTIONS.** This one basically speaks for itself. Executing the tasks you laid out will make up the bulk of this coaching phase. Make sure you stick to the instructions you gave yourself, and stay faithful to the timeline!

- **OBSTACLES.** This section, like the one above it, won't really come into play until you're well past the worksheet stage. As things unfold, keep an eye out for any warning signs that might develop into one of your predicted issues, and don't hesitate to take the appropriate countermeasures before things get out of hand!

- **SUCCESS**. This one's comparatively small, but important. All of your other planning went towards designing your coaching road map, but this step gives it a finish line. As you start to reach the end of your **Action** list, be more alert about the presence of whatever traits and qualities you associated with achieving your big goal. Once you get there, you're all done, and congratulations are in order for you and all your teammates—of course, it's also the perfect time to start the coaching process once more with a fresh goal, and see how much further you can go!

Accountability and Measuring Results

Knowing when you've crossed the finish line and achieved your **Success** is important, since it will give you a clear idea of when our step-by-step model has completed its cycle. That said, you'll also want a means of measuring success throughout the post-planning process, not just at the end. Besides giving you a consistent dose of healthy motivation, such knowledge is vital to determine whether or not a plan is proving to be effective in practice.

You may have noticed that measurement does not have its own dedicated spot on the worksheet—the reason for this is that it's a task that permeates the whole coaching process. Like the coaching **Skills and Behaviors** chapter from much earlier in this book, measuring results is such an inherent part of the coaching process that you'll benefit from practicing the associated behaviors in all areas of your business, not just during our process.

More than anything else, to effectively measure your plan's results, you need to have **Accountability**. What does it mean to be held accountable? To put it simply, accountability exists when one's responsibilities are clear and consequences (good, bad, or otherwise) exist. Accountability is the mark of a good leader, and of a good coach—it means you're a mature, dependable individual who can be counted on to treat all workplace situations with the proper respect.

So, how do you know you're properly holding yourself accountable, and how can you ensure that you maintain the behavior? A healthy place to start is the following list of questions, all of which you should freely and frequently ask yourself:

ACCOUNTABILITY QUESTIONS

- ➤ What exactly is the breakdown here? (vs. who's to blame)
- ➤ What can I do to solve the problem?
- ➤ What are some ways I can contribute?
- ➤ What can I do to make the project or team successful?
- ➤ How can I develop myself?
- ➤ How can I improve my performance?
- ➤ How can I influence others?

So, how does one become accountable? There are plenty of traits associated with accountability, but a few stand out as especially fundamental to the leaderly quality:

- **ENSURE ACCURACY.** First and foremost, being held accountable for your work means putting in your best effort to produce the best result possible. One of the most effective ways to improve quality is to proofread thoroughly. Go over everything before you submit your work, and consider letting your peers in on the process, as well, as another pair of eyes can often be all you need to pick out an otherwise-missed mistake.

- **MEET DEADLINES.** When you take full responsibility for your work, you're making an implicit commitment not only to maintain a standard of quality, but also to finish it on time. A strong awareness of deadlines leads to respect for a given project's size and scope, and will be necessary to get the most out of your **Action** list. As an added bonus, a leader who always meets deadlines will likely inspire teammates to strive for the same.

- **COMMUNICATE AND RESPOND.** Healthy communication in the workplace means not just listening to your teammates, but also providing consistent feedback, forming a legitimate dialogue. Review the "Feedback" section of the **Skills and Behaviors** chapter and put those ideas into practice whenever you're given the opportunity. If teammates find that you answer concerns with thoughtful, constructive responses, they'll come to see you as a respected, accountable authority figure.

- **HELP OTHERS.** An accountable leader understands his or her role in the team dynamic, and works as hard as anyone else to fulfill it. When you're in a position of authority, you have an obligation to see to not only your own individual duties, but those of your team, as well. Expect your teammates to do their best and pull their weight, but don't abandon them if they need your help. Support your peers, and you'll receive the same treatment in kind.

All that being said, what makes accountability so important to measuring results? Well, in the first place, following our coaching model, you'll need to be held accountable for your plans, actions, and business in general to achieve success, and even more so to measure it. Beyond that, with proper accountability comes a greater attention to detail within your business, which will allow you to more effectively gauge both your input and the effect it has on the big picture.

So, that's our first step. Build and maintain your sense of accountability, and your ability to measure results will naturally follow. Having come this far, what's the best way to measure results? It's a big question, so let's take the usual route of breaking it up into a few smaller ones:

- **WHAT DOES SUCCESS LOOK LIKE?** Feel free to draw inspiration from the **Success** section of the worksheet, but for this question, we're considering success as a broad concept, not just as a specific outcome to the coaching plan. Of course, you can tie it into your coaching plan, but try to focus on smaller sub-goals rather than your big one.

- **WHAT WILL I MEASURE TO DETERMINE SUCCESS?** Your answer will vary greatly depending on your role, your situation, and your answer to the previous question. There are plenty of ways to answer this question, but consider using the example below as inspiration to get you started.

- **HOW WILL I MEASURE?** First, you'll need to answer the above question, and then you'll need to do some research on what options you might have in terms of appropriate data-gathering tools, software, or the like. Again, you may find it helpful to refer to the example below.

Example: Measuring Success

What does Success Look Like? For example, increase individual growth by one achievement level per quarter.

What will I do to determine success? Achievement levels are pre-determined by corporate structure and are often represented by descriptions such as "bronze", "silver", "gold", and "platinum". Consult with corporate or upline to determine individual and team achievement levels. These are frequently recorded in real time and available online.

Content via Terri Kelly.

Ultimately, how you measure success will vary depending on the nature of your situation. That said, there are a few more general-purpose questions you can consider to find the right solution for you:

- **WHAT IS MY CURRENT LEVEL OF PERFORMANCE?** The easiest way to find and measure change in your business is to compare your current situation to a documented one in the past. Conveniently, the coaching worksheet you filled out can serve as such a document. Consider your responses and information, particularly your **Current Reality** section, and reflect back on the traits you weighed as important back then. Then, look for those traits and determine how they've changed since you first brainstormed.

- **WHAT SYSTEMS SHOULD I PUT IN PLACE?** It would be a very good idea to build new habits for consistently checking and recording your business' performance, if you aren't following them already. After you've finished your worksheet, try to implement relevant programs and behaviors early on. For example, if your goal were to improve customer satisfaction and encourage repeat visits, a logical and direct course of action would be to start giving customers surveys after you've done business.

- **HOW WILL I COMMUNICATE WITH EMPLOYEES?** For transparency's sake, it's good to keep your whole team aware of ongoing changes in your business' performance, especially in areas where they play a direct, active role.

- **HOW WILL I CELEBRATE SUCCESSES?** We're certainly big supporters of positive reinforcement. When business is doing well, you deserve to treat yourselves well! Be careful not to lose sight of your bigger goals or grow complacent, but an achieved success or milestone is certainly a worthy opportunity to give you and your team an appropriate reward. A regular announcement of positive results at team meetings is a great way to give everyone's spirits a boost.

Above all, stay alert for the little changes and impacts of the coaching plan in your business, and keep a positive attitude. Success is within your reach—keep striving for it, and you'll find yourself with something worth celebrating before you know it!

BRINGING IT ALL TOGETHER

Recommitting

The sun had just fully emerged from the horizon, and a steady stream of light shone into Wendy's bedroom. She jumped out of bed with anticipation. Even though she had worked late into the night, she vowed to make this the day that she recommitted to her team and her success. She was exhausted, but had an overwhelming feeling of satisfaction that she had completed the worksheet the night before. Her future looked bright and there was no time like the present to make some changes.

After pouring an extra strong cup of coffee, Wendy strolled into her home office and sat at the computer. After waiting for the system to boot up, she visited her company's website. She remembered how helpful and convincing the "Success Stories" tab had been when she first decided to quit her retail job and make the switch to direct sales. Seeing the potential and hearing all of the words of encouragement from people just like her had been what really sealed the deal for her. After all, if they could do it...so could she!

She spent most of the morning watching video after video. Some seemed as if they were written about her. Wendy was relieved to hear that her team wasn't the only team that struggled. She was more relieved to hear that most teams were able to overcome their obstacles and still become successful. She now knew that all of the time and energy she spent filling out the worksheet and answering the questions of her virtual coach were worthwhile. She was relieved, refreshed, and recommitted. Wendy called a team meeting.

The Big Picture

By now, you've experienced every level of our coaching model, from beginning to end. It may seem like a lot to absorb for now, but with just a little bit of practice, each step of the process will come to you naturally. In time, you may even find you can do it without the worksheet!

In the following chart, we've laid out each piece of the coaching model in their natural order.

COACHING MODEL

| Steps | ➡ | Behaviors | ➡ | Effects | ➡ | Results |

C	**Current Reality**			
	➢ What's working well?			
O	➢ What needs improvement?			
	Vision			
A	➢ What does it need to be/look like?			
	Action			
C	➢ How will we get there?	➢ Support	➢ Alignment	
	➢ What resources are needed?	➢ Commitment	➢ Motivation	➢ ROI
H	➢ What obstacles will get in the way?	➢ Encouragement	➢ Increased	➢ High
	➢ How will the obstacles be removed?	➢ Feedback	Capability	Performance
I	**Resources**	➢ Development		
	➢ What resources are needed?			
N	➢ What support do you need?			
	Obstacles			
G	➢ What blocks will get in your way?			
	➢ How will the obstacles be removed?			

Measurement Loop
➢ What does success look like?
➢ What is the desired outcome??

First, you enter the process with an overarching goal, represented on your worksheet by the **Topic** field. You keep this in mind throughout the execution of the plan, ensuring that your actions are laser-focused on future success!

The coaching process starts with your various brainstorming **Steps**, assisted by the worksheet: **Current Reality, Vision, Action, Resources,** and **Obstacles**. Next, you'll put your plan in motion, and make your ideas into reality through the various constructive **Behaviors** we addressed towards the beginning of this book. Once you have acted, you will be responsible for observing the **Effects**, and determining what they mean for your coaching strategy as you proceed—this will become a constant throughout the whole process, taking the form of a **Measurement Loop** as you grow accustomed to giving yourself and your plan honest, accurate feedback. Finally, if all goes well, you can enjoy the positive **Results** of your strategy.

Coaching leads to major growth and benefits, to be sure, but as you can see, it's a very simple, natural process! Keep practicing, and prepare yourself for each part of the process. In time, you may find yourself naturally applying our theories in all sorts of business situations—the more you familiarize yourself with the model now, the better off you'll be in the long run!

Review: What is Coaching?

As you may remember, we opened our discussion with this key question. Do you recall what came to mind when we raised the topic before? How has your understanding of the concept changed since then? Chances are it's expanded quite a bit!

In light of our full model, we think of coaching as an ongoing, mutually beneficial feedback loop between one or more parties. It challenges you to ask thought-provoking questions that inspire you or others to take action, ideally to achieve a specific result that's good for all involved. While our coaching model is flexible, we believe you'll find it most effective when it's applied to a one-on-one situation, or to a personal brainstorming session. The coaching expert can call upon the associated skills frequently and spontaneously, and as a result reaps great rewards in terms of performance, motivation, and participation.

How does this result come about? As a performance tool, coaching excels by providing immediate, specific feedback. By allowing yourself to be direct and transparent with both your questions and your answers, you'll get right to the material you want to address and can immediately get down to business in the areas that matter the most. As a motivational tool, coaching works by giving personal attention and recognition. By working with others on a small, one-on-one scale, you demonstrate that you're fully committed to them and are taking accountability for their success, inspiring all of your peers to work harder for the team's sake. As a participation tool, coaching succeeds by involving all active parties in their own growth and achievement, as well as that of the business. Opening up the playing field to all team members ensures that everyone gets back what he or she puts in, and is allowed to take responsibility for their own success.

What else makes coaching so effective? We've covered the basics, but there are plenty more convincing reasons where that came from:

- Coaching is focused, targeting a specific task or assignment at a given time. This ensures that you work on the issue you want, without anything else getting in the way!

- Coaching encourages direct observation and analysis of facts, so you can quickly pinpoint and understand the results of your actions.

- Coaching lends itself to a friendly, helpful atmosphere in the workplace. The success of your actions will inspire others to follow your good example, spreading the positivity all around!

- Finally, it may take some practice, but with time, coaching is very easy to understand and adopt in all sorts of situations, and fosters a self-sustaining growth trend. The more coaching you do, the better at coaching you'll be; growth will beget growth, and you'll reap exponential rewards!

Sustainability – Where Will Coaching Take You Next?

Of course, we're happy to provide you with all the advice we can give, but ultimately, you'll achieve the best possible outcome of our coaching process once you've learned to do it without our support. You know what they say about giving a person a fish versus teaching them to fish—we aim to teach you to coach, not only so that you can experience growth and success in your business, but also so that you can apply it to others, and teach them in turn. Together, we can turn coaching into a widespread renewable resource!

The best way to do this, as we've emphasized throughout this book, is to practice, practice, and then practice some more for good measure.

Really, you should never stop practicing—you may feel as though success and skill mastery mean never having to practice again, but what they actually mean is that you're now able to learn far more numerous and complex concepts than you could when you started. The more you practice, the more you'll learn, and the more you'll be able to pass on to others.

We think of learning as a constant ongoing process with no true end result, but that doesn't mean the process can't have milestones and little "finish lines" along the way. Every now and then, as you keep practicing the coaching model, you'll find it helpful to pause, take an objective stance, and evaluate where you are compared to where you were last time you checked. Engage in a personal feedback loop, asking yourself some key questions—out of the behaviors you've been practicing, what works particularly well, and what needs improvement? What should you stop doing, what should you start doing, and what should you keep doing just like you have been? All in all, what can you still get out of the process that you haven't already, and how far do you believe you can get by the time of your next self-evaluation?

Lastly, you'll find that your quest towards coaching mastery will be most easily achieved if you allow the process to be a true team effort. Invite your teammates into the process whenever they're available and willing to help, and always keep yourself open to feedback. Furthermore, take your teammates' feedback seriously, and see how you can build off of it to improve even further. The road to self-sustaining coaching may be long, but knowing you don't have to make the trip alone makes the journey that much richer and more rewarding!

EPILOGUE – WENDY

The American Dream Comes True

She may have stumbled upon it just on a whim, but Wendy sure owes a lot to the coaching model. You saw how effectively and amicably she cleared up the issues with her team, and things only got better from there—once Wendy got the ball rolling, there was nothing that could keep her from her dream of major business success. Today, she's earned the respect of all of her teammates, and her team has doubled in size since Wendy recommitted to the team success.

With the added growth to the team, Wendy now has even more time to give to her family and friends. In fact, she is planning a week-long family vacation next month – something she has dreamt about for years. See, the retail world wouldn't allow her to take a week off. Now that she was in control of her own success, the week is hers!

I bet you saw a bit of yourself in Wendy because not only is Wendy relatable, she represents a great percentage of the population. By following our plan and worksheet, practicing productive behaviors, and promoting a group dynamic of teamwork and feedback, you, too, can achieve success. With time and practice, coaching will become a key component of your business technique, and you'll see the results in plain view on a daily basis.

That's all there is to it, dear reader. It's true, it's that simple! So, what are you waiting for? Review our advice, run through the worksheet, and download our workbook for further study. Practice, practice, practice— and above all, happy coaching!

www.ingramcontent.com/pod-product-compliance
Lightning Source LLC
Chambersburg PA
CBHW071758170526
45167CB00003B/1078